Joe makes a house

Story by Annette Smith
Illustrations by Meredith Thomas

Katie went to play with Anna.

The girls played
with Anna's new doll's house.

"The little table and chairs
can go here," said Katie.

At home, Katie said to Joe,
"I **did** like Anna's doll's house."

"I can make a doll's house for you,"
said Joe.
"I will find some boxes."

Joe came back with three boxes.

He made a house.

It had three rooms.

"Here you are, Katie," said Joe.

"This will make a good roof."

Katie said,

"It can go on top of the doll's house.

I can paint it yellow."

Katie said,

"Look at the roof, Joe!"

Joe painted some windows
on the outside of the house.

Katie made a little table, and Mom helped her make two little chairs.

"They can go down here in this room," said Katie.

"Now I will make some beds,"
said Katie.

She got some little boxes.

"My little teddy and the dolls
can sleep in the beds," she said.
"They can go up here."

"I love this doll's house,"
said Katie. "Thank you, Joe."